CATOLOGY

This edition printed in 2021
By SJG Publishing, HP22 6NF, UK

All rights reserved. No part of this work may be reproduced in any form or by any means, electronic or mechanical, including photocopying, recording or by any information storage and retrieval system, without the prior written permission of the publisher.

© Susanna Geoghegan Gift Publishing

Author: Michael Powell
Cover design: Milestone Creative
Contents design: seagulls.net

ISBN: 978-1-913004-15-6

Printed in China

10 9 8 7 6 5 4 3 2 1

Contents

Introduction	4
It's a cat's life in your hands	6
Your cat's emotional world	9
The bonding touch	12
Why play is important	15
Social skills	18
How clever are cats?	21
Rude? How to respect your cat's boundaries	24
How do cats learn?	27
Train your cat	30
Environmental enrichment	33
Memory, all alone in the moonlight	36
It's all in the eyes	39
Telltale tails	42
Extraordinary senses	45
Ears in action	48
How many whiskers does a cat have?	51
A medley of meows	54
Body language	58
Eight things you should know about your cat's hunting	63
Grooming	66
Ten things you should know about litter trays	69
Rubbing and scenting	72
Clues your cat loves you	75
Problem behaviour	78
Stress, anxiety and depression	81
Signs your cat is unwell	84
Elderly cats	88
Twenty things you should know about cats	91
What can we learn from cats?	94

Introduction

Catology is the art and science of the mind and behaviour, instincts and intentions, hopes and dreams, caprice, kinks and machinations of the domesticated carnivoran of the family Felidae, *otherwise known as – our crazy-cute, lovably-aloof, clean-freak fur balls – cats.*

At home, at work or at play, on the sofa or lying sprawled along the top of a radiator having a micro-nap, anyone can become an expert catologist, so long as they have an open and loving heart, the curiosity to learn about the mysterious feline psyche and a willingness to view the world from a cat's perspective.

We hope this little book will encourage you to understand, communicate more effectively with, and nurture all the cats in your life, during the short time you spend together. We also hope that it fuels a burning desire to help them to be healthy, happy and, above all, – uniquely themselves.

IT'S A CAT'S LIFE IN YOUR *HANDS*

Cat owners strive to give their cats the best care possible during the relatively short time that they share our lives. They join our families, destroy our furniture, fill up our hearts and then, all too soon, it's time for them to cross the 'rainbow bridge'. So, what is the single most important way to enrich your feline friend's daily experience while you enjoy this precious time together?

Actually, the answer is very simple, but it's not what you might think. We all want our pets to have a rich, safe, happy and long life. The key is how to achieve all those things. For example, the answer isn't 'love your cat unconditionally', nor is it 'invest in a mega scratching post activity centre and clean out the litter tray twice a day'. You can't love an animal and do what's best for him without a knowledge base, but, equally, your cat needs more than having its functional needs fulfilled. Unlike a domesticated dog, your cat is an evolutionary free agent, so living in a modern home is a considerable compromise. As Abigail Tucker observes in her book, *The Lion in the Living Room*, 'For while cats cozy up to humans, sitting pretty in our settlements … they don't *need* to remain among us. They are still cats after all. They can always step back into what's left of the wild'.

One of the most important things you can do is to try to see things from your cat's point of view, to understand what he wants and needs. An essential part of this is to maintain what cat behaviourist star of the hit TV show *My Cat From Hell* and author of *Total Cat Mojo*, Jackson Galaxy, calls an 'insistence at seeing the rawness in your cat at all times'. We cat lovers think we know lots about cats just because we love them and assume that's more than halfway to understanding them. But the truth is that sometimes the way we treat our animals, often with the best intentions, is just plain wrong. For example, many cat owners, either verbally or physically, punish their cats for bringing prey they have caught into the house, for spraying on the sofa, or for pulling food out of the bowl and making a mess on the kitchen floor.

> We cat lovers think we know lots about cats just because we love them

A cat who brings you his prey isn't a bad cat – he's actually a very good cat who is showing trust and affection. A cat who sprays on the sofa isn't being wilfully naughty or deliberately confrontational – it's a sign that he is feeling territorial anxiety and needs to calm himself down by spreading his own scent around the house. If your cat pulls food out of his bowl, it could be because the bowl is too narrow and he doesn't like the unpleasant feeling of his whiskers brushing against it; or it might be in the wrong location – in a noisy thoroughfare, or too close to the litter tray – it's your job to figure out the reason rather than to scold him.

So, how do we become less prone to making these mistakes? By keeping building our knowledge base whilst recognising more fully the differences between our two species, rather than winging it with a nurturing instinct and best intentions. Some of the information in this book will confirm what you already know, but it will also help you become aware of some of your misconceptions. Abigail Tucker again: 'A house cat is not really a fur baby, but is something rather more remarkable: a tiny conquistador with the whole planet at its feet. House cats would not exist without humans, but we didn't really create them, nor do we control them now. Our relationship is less about ownership than aiding and abetting'.

> A cat who brings you his prey isn't a bad cat – he's actually a very good cat

YOUR CAT'S EMOTIONAL WORLD

You don't have to be a cat owner to believe that cats have emotions, even though for the purposes of survival they remain very adept at hiding most of them, except for fear and anger. Nevertheless, it seems obvious to us that cats have an emotional inner life, but not everybody agrees.

In his book, *Cat Sense*, John Bradshaw observes: 'In scientific circles, it has only recently become acceptable to talk about animal emotions, and one school of thought still maintains that emotions are a by-product of consciousness' and therefore that cats and dogs cannot possess them. Bradshaw agrees with the wide consensus that 'emotions are a necessary component of the mechanisms that drive animal behaviour' although he concedes that cats are 'masters at concealing their thoughts, and are even better at hiding their emotions'.

Millennia ago, when we were living in the earliest agrarian communities and were more in touch with the natural world, humans formed close relationships with dogs. The existence of their emotions would have been self-evident, just as it is for us today. But our relationship with cats has been different until very recently.

Living in stable tightly-bonded groups is predicated on the ability to express emotions and to read body language and predict the intentions of others. Dogs and humans are both social animals and therefore they possess these skills. But cats are solitary. In the wild, a male cat lives alone, so a capacity to express and read emotions does not confer an evolutionary advantage.

Although cats and humans have an association dating back over 10,000 years, when early farmers used the tamer wildcats to control vermin in their grain stores, these cats didn't need to co-operate and communicate with humans for their food and shelter in the way that proto-dogs did.

Even today, people who dislike cats will cite their independence and emotional indifference as unlikeable traits (although many cat lovers claim that they are drawn to them precisely because of these qualities, and that dogs are too needy and ingratiating). It is well known that during the Middle Ages, the Roman Catholic Church persecuted cats because of their association with paganism and witchcraft, but it is highly probable that their independence, solitary natures and inscrutability were contributory factors.

Cats simply aren't as emotionally accessible as dogs because the way the relationship between cats and humans has developed over the last several thousand years has not required them to be. They may be fully domesticated today and rely on us for their food and shelter but, from an evolutionary perspective, they have had a mere fraction of the time that dogs have enjoyed to deepen their emotional connection with humans.

Nevertheless, it is undeniable that cats can form a strong attachment to their owners (as all cat lovers know). Today, with our understanding of modern neurochemistry, we know that cats possess some of the same brain structures and chemistry that produce emotions in humans, such as the neurotransmitter serotonin and the stress hormone cortisol. We also know that levels of the 'love' hormone oxytocin increase in humans and cats when we spend time together (although dogs produce about five times more than cats).

Research has shown that cat owners differ considerably on the range of emotions that they attribute to their cats. A 2008 survey showed that nearly all of them believed that their cats could feel curiosity, affection, joy and fear; more than 80% credited them with surprise and anger; but nearly a third of owners were unsure whether their cats were capable of feeling anxiety or sadness.

John Bradshaw aptly sums up the cat's emotional world: 'Cats' emotional lives are more elaborate than their detractors would have us think, but not quite as sophisticated as the most ardent cat-lover would probably like to believe'.

THE BONDING
Touch

It is important for a kitten's socialisation with humans that he is handled regularly during the first eight weeks of his life (and beyond) and is exposed to a wide variety of people during those crucial early weeks so he gets used to being picked up and handled by them.

Your cat has areas of his body that are more sensitive, or are more sensitive to touch, than others. You should learn where they are and respect his preferences. The most vulnerable area of a cat's body is the tummy, which is why he will only lie on his back with his belly exposed when he feels very comfortable and trusting. That's probably not an invitation for you to dive in with your big clumsy hands to rub his tummy though.

Most kittens like to play fight using nails and teeth. Even though his tiny teeth can't hurt your hands, use toys for fighting and hunting games, rather than your own body, otherwise you will teach him that it's acceptable to bite and claw humans. Getting him to stalk and pounce on your toes under a duvet can be fun at first, but five years later you may be thoroughly fed up with his insistence on policing even the slightest duvet movement.

Paw pads are another sensitive body part. They contain lots of nerve endings that enable your cat to literally to feel the ground, or the subtle movements of their prey, and they are important for cushioning and balance. Cats also sweat through their feet. You shouldn't play with your cat's paw pads just for fun, but he should become accustomed to you inspecting them regularly to make sure they're clean and free from injury (cracks, cuts, abrasions, bleeding or swelling).

Most cats love being stroked and tickled around the head and will push their heads hard against your hands as you stroke them. Other favourite spots include the cheeks and behind the ears. Avoid touching the whiskers – located on the muzzle, above the eyes, under the chin and on the wrists behind the front paws – as these are highly sensitive.

The correct way to pick up your cat is to place one hand around his chest and under his front legs and steady him with the other hand as you bring him towards your chest. Support his whole body as you hold him against your chest and make sure you don't leave any legs dangling or he'll start using his claws to find stability. Hold your cat firmly but gently and always put him down the moment he starts to wriggle or flick his tail.

According to John Alderton, author of *Understanding Your Cat*, 'A cat's breed affects the kind of companionship that it prefers'. In *The Cat Whisperer*, Claire Bessant claims that a researcher in the US 'has recognised two different types of feline character within the groups of kittens she has studied … excitable and nervous, and those which are much more relaxed and quiet in their attitude to life and its challenges'.

She believes this applies to cats in their adult life too: 'Current work on the personality of the adult cat … points to the likelihood of there being two different and distinct types'. She describes type one as needing 'lots of social contact with both people and other cats and is relaxed in their company'. The second type 'seems only to enjoy the company of one or two members of its human family … and often doesn't form bonds with other cats either'.

Bessant says that animal behaviourists do not yet fully understand the extent to which nature and nurture have produced these two personality types. A type two cat generally won't initiate contact and visitors usually get short shrift. It is even more important that you cuddle and interact physically with this type on his own terms, otherwise you'll end up with a stressed pet that avoids human contact at all costs. If you have a cat like this, you can stop blaming yourself for his apparent lack of socialisation; he may just have been born this way.

WHY PLAY IS *IMPORTANT*

In his book, Total Cat Mojo, *Jackson Galaxy uses the acronym HCKEGS to remind cat owners of the basic innate drives that must be satisfied for a domestic cat to lead a happy and fulfilled life. It stands for Hunt, Catch, Kill, Eat, Groom, Sleep. Notice how much of a cat's driving force is linked to hunting. Your cat is a natural-born hunter and those instincts don't disappear just because he spends most of his life lying on the sofa with you.*

Catology

For thousands of years we depended on cats to kill vermin in our grain stores and in some ancient cultures, such as in Egypt, cats were worshipped for their ability to exterminate pests. We've only really moved from a rural model to an urban model in the last 250 years, and bringing cats inside to share our homes is more recent still – credited to Queen Victoria's love of dogs and cats.

Cats make a huge compromise to live with humans. They limit their freedom of movement, they share their territory, eat what we feed them and they even have to scratch and do their business where we decide. So, when your cat trots proudly into the house with a dead squirrel in its mouth, you should cut him some slack.

If your cat goes outdoors, it's natural for him to come back with prey he has caught – and it may well be alive. Mothers do this to teach their kittens how to hunt. You should view it as an act of affection and trust, rather than punish your cat for turning feral. There's no point telling him off, because that will only leave him confused, and you definitely don't want to pile on the praise either, so your best option is to calmly remove the dead or dying animal and then distract your cat with some food.

As Jackson Galaxy is keen to emphasise, a brush with your cat's live prey reminds you that: 'play isn't a luxury, something that is a fun diversion if and when you have time ... If you have a cat, you have interactive toys and you use them for daily play sessions ... they are a physical and behavioural necessity'.

> **Play isn't a luxury, something that is a fun diversion if and when you have time**

Regardless of whether your cat is in the habit of dragging semi-conscious rodents into your house, it is your responsibility and daily duty to give your cat structured play hunting sessions for the sake of his psychological and physical wellbeing. It's not something you do every now and again when you're feeling a bit bored, or guilty that you have been too busy to give your cat the attention he needs.

Jackson Galaxy cannot stress enough that 'play is a structured activity'. It requires your commitment and your focus as you guide your cat through a re-enactment of the hunting process. It isn't simply a matter of making your cat tear around the room, always keeping him frustratingly short of catching his prey. There will be moments when your cat's feather toy lies motionless on the floor, quivering slightly as he stalks it with maximum concentration and starts to wind himself up to a pounce and kill action.

> Scientific research has revealed that cats do treat toys just like they do prey

Playing hunting games with your cat should be like a symphony, with all its variety of moods and tempos, rather than a minute waltz, rushed and frantic and over all too soon because you've got more important things to do. Being a responsible cat owner means channelling these and other behaviours in a structured way, to give your cat security and consistency so that you can all live happily together under the same roof without repressing his natural instincts.

They may be toys to us 'but cats regard them more seriously than the word implies', observe John Bradshaw and Sarah Ellis in their book, *The Trainable Cat*. 'In fact, scientific research has revealed that cats do treat toys just like they do prey … so it seems likely that when they are playing, they think that the "toy" is actually prey'.

SOCIAL
Skills

By their nature, cats are solitary creatures. In the wild, male cats live alone and they hunt alone. Their fierce independence has earned all cats a reputation for having zero social skills. Which simply isn't true. In feral conditions, female cats live in groups consisting mainly of queens and their litters – multiple generations of related females living together and rearing kittens communally.

Social Skills

Cats can read each other's body language (see page 58) and they use a variety of vocalisations to communicate with each other. They also use a medley of meows that are solely reserved for communicating with humans (see page 57). But, because they are independent and appear only to tolerate interaction with humans and other animals on their own terms, they are often labelled as disinterested and socially inept.

The truth is, there are plenty of opportunities for you to interact positively and sociably with your cat. Cats are sociable animals to a point, not to the same extent as dogs, but still better than nearly all other domesticated animals. Domestic dogs are very skilled at reading human social and communicative behaviour – even more so than our nearest primate relatives (and even some of our human relatives!). Cats apparently, not so much, but their ability to learn how to interact with other species is still very impressive.

In *Cat Sense*, John Bradshaw explains: 'Cats, like dogs, are capable of multiple socialization, the ability to become attached to animals of several different species – and not just people and other cats. Kittens raised in a household with a cat-friendly dog will continue to be friendly towards that dog, and potentially other similar dogs, for their entire lives'. Bradshaw speculates that cats are able to 'keep the "rules" for interacting with each separate species in discrete parts of their brains' and he also praises a cat's 'behavioural flexibility' for being plucked from its mother and siblings after eight weeks and then being able to forge new attachments in a stranger's home.

The window is quite narrow for socialising kittens; they form their view of humans between the ages of four and eight weeks, so to create an approachable cat it is important to expose her to a wide variety of people during those crucial early weeks and get her used to being picked up and handled by them.

If a kitten is raised in a household of exclusively adult women during her first two months, she may become fearful of men and children after she has been homed. Likewise, if during this time a single person has been responsible for most of her care, she will become overly attached to that person and initially find it hard to become optimally socialised to other humans.

Studies of rescued kittens that have been deprived of human contact have shown that so long as these semi-feral animals are handled (and preferably receive extra human intervention) before they reach nine weeks of age, they can catch up to become happy well-socialised pets. 'Kittens that don't meet a human until the age of ten weeks or older', says John Bradshaw, 'are unlikely to become pets, except in extreme circumstances. Instead, they live as "stray" or "feral" cats, living on the fringes of human activity but never becoming part of it'.

> Successful socialisation has wide-reaching consequences

Successful socialisation has wide-reaching consequences that impact the rest of a cat's life. Its long term health and wellbeing rest with your ability as owner to understand your cat's needs so that you can provide what cat experts call 'environmental enrichment' (see page 33).

This has been the primary focus of veterinary scientists such as Emeritus Professor of Veterinary Clinical Sciences at Ohio State University, Dr Tony Buffington, who believes that the realisation of the importance of the human/animal relationship on animal health and the imperative of equipping pet owners with the information needed to create an environment that permits pets to thrive, has been the biggest advance in veterinary medicine in the past ten years.

HOW CLEVER ARE CATS?

People often cite the benchmark of a two-and-a-half-year-old human child when discussing the intelligence of cats. However, cats are less attentive towards humans and more susceptible to stress than dogs, which poses major obstacles for intelligence testing.

Despite this, cats have been tested by many of the standard benchmarks, such as 'object permanence', 'physical causality' and 'quantity discrimination', and they certainly have prodigious memories.

Object permanence: As far back as the 1970s, scientists reported that cats demonstrated four of the six stages of object permanence – the idea that when an object is out of sight, the subject realises that it still exists – established by Swiss psychologist Jean Piaget in his work with children. Human babies normally reach Stage Six before the age of two. Stage Four involves retrieving hidden objects. In an 'invisible displacement test', an experimenter shows a cat their food being hidden in a container, which is then placed behind a screen. The experimenter then shows the cat an empty container. Most cats look behind the screen, reasoning correctly that the food is still there.

Physical causality: The standard test for understanding physical causality involves putting food on the end of various bits of string and then observing whether the subject pulls the correct one. In one experiment, fifteen cats were presented with three set-ups: a single string with food at the other end; two parallel strings, only one of which was baited; and two crossed strings with one baited. All the cats managed to pull the single string to reach the food but none of them performed better than chance on the other two tasks, giving no evidence that cats understand the function of the strings or their physical causality.

Quantity discrimination: In tests where domestic cats are offered two different quantities of food, they tend to choose the larger quantity more often than the smaller one, even when the food is hidden from view, proving that they are capable of spontaneously discriminating quantities and that they mainly use visual cues (rather than smell, for example).

Memory: Tests have shown that a cat's ability to retain information is superior to that of other domestic animals. In research by Dr Norman Maier, professor of psychology at the University of Michigan, and Dr Schneirla, curator at the Department of Animal Behaviour, American Museum of Natural History, cats and dogs were shown a variety of boxes and were taught that the presence of food underneath a box was indicated by a glowing light bulb on top. Cats were able to remember which box contained the food for as long as sixteen hours after seeing the light bulb, whereas dogs couldn't retain this information for much longer than five minutes.

Are cats smarter than dogs?

Another question that many dog owners think they already know the answer to is: are cats smarter than dogs? Because dogs have a reputation for being easier to train than cats, this has helped to create the idea that dogs are more intelligent. But 'experiments have shown that dogs are more attentive to human gestures than even chimpanzees, supposedly the most intelligent of all the animals, apart from ourselves', say John Bradshaw and Sarah Ellis, which means that 'training a dog will always be different from training any other animal'. Cats and dogs are, in fact, equally capable of learning and learn in the same way, but cats are less motivated.

Bearing all this in mind, a team led by neurologist Suzana Herculano-Houzel used a novel post-mortem technique to estimate the number of neurons in the cerebral cortex of animal brains (which renders irrelevant the question of motivation and attentiveness). They counted 500 million neurons in a dog's brain, which is double the 250 million they measured in the brains of cats, and concluded that dogs are the smarter species. Humans have 16 billion, in case you were wondering.

RUDE? HOW TO RESPECT YOUR CAT'S *Boundaries*

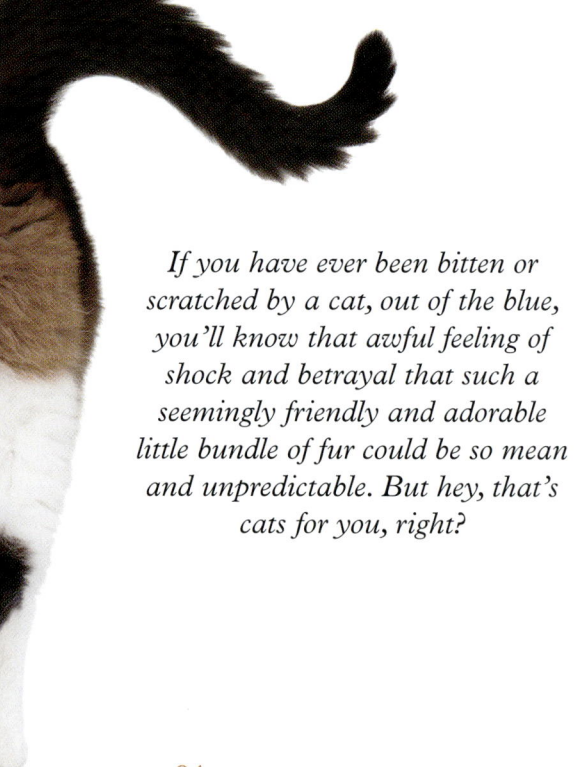

If you have ever been bitten or scratched by a cat, out of the blue, you'll know that awful feeling of shock and betrayal that such a seemingly friendly and adorable little bundle of fur could be so mean and unpredictable. But hey, that's cats for you, right?

Rude? How to Respect Your Cat's Boundaries

Sounds familiar? Of course, you're wrong. Cats are no less predictable than any other domestic animal, so long as you respect their boundaries and learn to read their subtle (and not so subtle) warnings whenever you overstep the mark.

No matter how much your cat appears to enjoy your company, you must always remember to interact on his terms, so you never overstay your welcome. This doesn't mean being a pushover and letting your cat run the household; it's about showing respect for your cat as an autonomous independent being, rather than a fluffy plaything that should always be available for your amusement. Here are five familiar scenarios where humans often come unstuck:

> It's about showing respect for your cat as an autonomous independent being

1. Tummy tickling: You're enjoying a nice petting session, the cat's purring like a lawnmower and nuzzling his cheek against the back of your hand, really enjoying the attention. Suddenly he rolls onto his back and exposes his belly to you, which you interpret as an open invitation to clumsily rub and tickle. So, you oblige and he claws you. When a cat exposes his belly to you, it's an indication that he feels very comfortable with you, but it is rarely an invitation to touch the most vulnerable part of his body. Take the compliment but don't abuse his trust.

2. So irresistible when they're asleep: Your cat is sleeping curled up on the sofa like a hairy doughnut, tail and paws together, tail tucked around, chin facing the ceiling. You can't resist petting him gently and, with a high-pitched whine, asking if he's having a lovely sleep. He turns his head, meows with irritation and then stomps off to find somewhere else to sleep undisturbed. Who's the rude one in this scenario? When was the last time you appreciated someone waking you up?

3. Sometimes, hello is enough: Your cat silently enters the room, trots towards you with his tail in the air, ears pricked, eyes wide and happy. He rubs against your leg and lets out a little meow. That's when you notice him, pick him up and smother him with affection. He struggles to get free and you feel rebuffed. If you'd been paying attention, you'd have noticed that your cat actually said 'How's it going?' *three times*, but you just had to escalate it into a full on bear hug. 'Why can't you just be cool?' thinks your cat. 'Why do you have to act like I've been missing for a fortnight?'

4. Don't force your cat into an uncomfortable situation: You have guests. They bring their small dog and two young children. Everyone is dying to meet your cat and make friends. Your cat has slipped quietly away and is hiding under a wardrobe at the far end of the house, so you fetch him and everyone has lots of rambunctious fun getting to know each other. Except, this is not a situation your cat needed any part of. Why did you disrespect his natural instincts and put him in such a vulnerable position?

5. Stop when he's had enough: He's lying on your chest and you're having a nuzzle. He's been rubbing his head into your face, so you're both feeling pretty loved up. Two minutes later, he starts to swish his tail, which is a sign that he's ready to move on with his busy schedule, but you pull him closer for another cuddle. His body language makes it very clear that he's had enough, but you ignore all the signs. So, he clamps his claws onto your arm. If you want a more rewarding relationship with your cat, stop being so needy and he'll come looking for more affection in the longer-term.

HOW DO CATS *Learn?*

Cats, like dogs and children, learn best by positive reinforcement, a simple technique that rewards desired ('good') behaviour and ignores undesirable ('bad') behaviour. This seems obvious, but many cat owners actually create and then reinforce the conditions that have caused the problem behaviour in the first place, and then resort to punishment, which only creates a fearful and confused cat.

Whether you want to teach your cat a domestic life skill (such as swallowing a worming pill) or stop him from doing something, it's important to understand that cats respond to praise and positive reinforcement but they do not react favourably to force of any kind. This includes physical punishment, squirting with water and loud verbal admonishment. Dr Tony Buffington is not exaggerating when he says, 'We tend to see shouting and punishment as forms of "conflict resolution"; cats see these as life-threatening'.

Even if fear were an acceptable form of correction (which it isn't), reprimands and punishments only work if you catch your cat in the act of doing something 'bad' and respond immediately. Any punishment that comes even a few seconds after the event will still traumatise your cat, but he won't connect it with the undesirable behaviour. So, you are left with the worst of outcomes – a terrified, confused cat that still performs what you see as problem behaviour. Dr Buffington advises: 'If you do catch your cat making a mistake, it is better for both of you to create a distraction by making a loud noise or throwing something (NOT at the cat!) that will attract its attention, but not toward you'.

Any punishment that comes even a few seconds after the event will still traumatise your cat

The key to learning is good communication and this doesn't just mean barking orders and bending your cat to your will. Your first instinct should be to try to figure out why your cat is behaving in a certain way. As you learn more about a cat's needs, you will realise that there is a explanation for nearly every kind of behaviour and even the most bizarre can usually be classified in three ways, none of which are the cat's fault:

How Do Cats Learn?

1. It is 'natural' in so far as the cat is following its natural instincts, but the situation requires your gentle intervention in order to make it tolerable. For example, cats naturally have a different sleep-wake cycle to humans, so your cat might run around the house at night in hunting mode. It sounds like he's dragging a sack full of rocks up and down the stairs and it keeps you awake. You might be able to decrease this nocturnal hunting by adding more playful activities to his daytime routine.

2. It is your cat's inevitable, logical and natural response to a dysfunctional environment. For example, he keeps going to the toilet on the sofa instead of the litter tray. To fix this, you need to figure out what is wrong with the litter tray. It might be too big, too small, in the wrong place (too noisy, not enough privacy, not easily accessible), too dirty (you don't keep it clean), or the wrong kind of litter (most cats prefer fine-grained, unscented litters).

3. It is a sign that he feels threatened by something in his environment (e.g. the litter tray is clean and perfectly positioned, but a new aggressive cat in the neighbourhood is making him highly anxious) or your cat is unwell (see a vet, pronto).

Apart from avoiding problem behaviour, why train a cat at all? Throughout your cat's life, you will encounter situations that will require your intervention to help him to learn a new skill: for example, to feel safe and comfortable in a cat carrier for trips to the vet; taking medication; being groomed; and adapting to change such as a new pet or baby in the household. It's a vast subject, but the next chapter tackles some of the key principles of positive reinforcement.

TRAIN YOUR *Cat*

To some ears, cat training sounds as ludicrous as a flea circus, but actually cats are fantastic learners and there will be many times when they can benefit – not from 'obedience training' but from acquiring a new skill, such as taking a tablet, enjoying a visit to the vet, feeling at home in a carrier or welcoming a new addition to the household.

This section introduces some of the broader principles of cat training, but if you want to explore this subject in the necessary detail, read *The Trainable Cat* by John Bradshaw and Sarah Ellis, who say: 'The primary purpose in training a pet cat should always be improving the cat's own sense of well-being, although owners will also find that at the same time they will reap the considerable reward of having a happier, easier to manage cat'.

The major problem with trying to train a cat is that her natural reaction to a break of routine, something that she might find potentially aversive, is to *run away*. 'For this reason,' say Bradshaw and Ellis, 'training often has to start with changes to the cat's environment that enhance its general feelings of security, giving the cat enough confidence to face its fears, albeit in a much more dilute form,' after which the trainer can begin to build up positive associations around the unfamiliar experience.

Before any training begins, your cat needs to feel calm and secure, so you need to set up a good learning environment, somewhere familiar, free from noise and bustle and distractions (e.g. if your training takes place next to a big window with a prime view of the bird feeder, your feline pupil is unlikely to pay you much attention). Bradshaw and Ellis recommend that the rewards should come 'little and often': little so eating doesn't interrupt the momentum of the training or fill up the cat too quickly, and often so that you can deliver lots of rewards (cooked meat or fish is best). Each morsel should be about 'half the size of your smallest fingernail'.

The basic philosophy behind all cat training is *positive reinforcement:* 'to reward desired behaviour and ignore unwanted behaviour or redirect it toward a more appropriate target'. The reward should follow immediately after the cat performs the desired behaviour, otherwise she won't make the connection.

In their book, Bradshaw and Ellis explain in extensive detail the nine key skills that form their foundation for training cats. Here is a very brief summary:

1. Reward spontaneous observation and exploration: e.g. if your cat spontaneously explores a new cat carrier (rather than you plonk her down near it), you reward her every time.

2. Systematic desensitisation and counter conditioning.

3. Luring: enticing the cat into a new situation with a reward.

4. Marking a behaviour: using verbal praise or a mechanical clicker when you can't reward immediately because you're too far away.

5. Touch-release-reward: e.g. you need to inspect the cat's ear, so you touch the ear, release, then give your cat a reward to build positive associations with being touched in an unfamiliar place.

6. Teaching relaxation: this involves creating a link between a blanket and relaxation, so the blanket can be used as a relaxation aid in unfamiliar surroundings.

7. Collecting the cat's scent: (using a glove or hair from her hairbrush) and then wiping it on unfamiliar items so that she will more readily accept them.

8. Maintaining a taught behaviour: initially rewarding every time you get the desired response (continuous reinforcement) and then gradually phasing this out once the desired behaviour has become consistent and reliable.

9. Recognising the optimal time to end the training session: when it's going badly, better to end it rather than drag it out; when it's going well, stop while the cat is still feeling motivated and interested.

ENVIRONMENTAL
Enrichment

Cats make a huge compromise to live inside our homes, so creating an environment that stimulates your cat's senses, makes her feel safe and gives her opportunities to exercise her natural instincts is paramount, especially for indoor cats.

Your cat will only thrive if the environment meets her physical, psychological and emotional needs. Dr Tony Buffington from Ohio State University has spent his career studying the human-animal bond and the effects of the environment on health in pets. He has treated hundreds of animals that have developed chronic illnesses that he attributes to a lack of environmental enrichment.

'If we are going to assert the authority to confine animals, then we have to accept the responsibility of doing it in as enriched a way as possible,' says Dr Buffington. His strategy involves firstly addressing the basic cat needs, understanding the things she needs to do, and then identifying 'feline life stressors', the common situations that affect a cat's health and welfare.

His most important guiding principles are never to use force, to reward desirable behaviour and distract a cat from undesirable behaviour rather than punish; wherever possible to give your cat a sense of control (e.g. if changing the position of a litter tray, leave the old one in place, so your cat can choose); and to remove anything in the environment that could make your cat feel stressed or threatened.

Basic cat needs: you should already be familiar with these, but here is a quick checklist.

- A room or other space she can call her own, with food and water, a bed, litter tray (at least one per cat), scratching/climbing post/s, a window to look out of and some toys. This should be a safe quiet space where she can't be snuck up on or ambushed, not a thoroughfare.

- Water fresh, in a shallow bowl, changed and cleaned regularly; litter tray in a private safe place, also changed and cleaned regularly. Several places to hide, climb up high, rest and sleep – where she can feel safe from people, loud noises and other animals.

Environmental Enrichment

Understanding cats: Dr Buffington's summary is: 'The keys to enjoying cats in our lives are to: 1. Provide acceptable outlets for them to "do what they need to do", and 2. Protect them from threats'.

For example, cats have a different daily sleep-wake to ours that involves resting and sleeping interspersed with many bursts of hunting activity (in the wild, a cat must catch as many as 10 small prey each day). That's why your cat runs around sporadically during the night when you are trying to sleep. Understanding this instinct, rather than trying to suppress it, keeps your cat happy and ideally helps you to accommodate her needs rather than lose your temper.

Every time your cat does something that inconveniences you in some way, instead of punishing her, you first need to understand why she is doing it (the answer is often 'because she needs to – it's her natural behaviour'). For example, if she keeps jumping up on top of the wardrobe where you keep your priceless collection of Toby jugs, understand that sometimes she *needs* to be up high to feel safe, so any breakages are not her personal comment on your taste in pottery. Move the jugs – problem solved.

Feline life stressors: 'Life stressors are events and changes in your cat's environment that may affect her well-being' says Dr Buffington. 'Our research suggests that some cats are unusually sensitive to their surroundings'. So be alert to any change in your cat's normal environment that could cause her stress. It could be something major, such as a new person or pet moving in or leaving, or as seemingly trivial as entertaining guests or moving furniture. The stakes are high, so avoid, identify and eliminate or adapt these stressors before your cat becomes nervous, fearful, develops behavioural problems such as aggression, or becomes chronically sick.

MEMORY, ALL ALONE IN THE *MOONLIGHT*

Much like Grizabella, who sings her famous aria in the musical Cats, *domestic cats recall the good times and the bad times, in other words, their information-retention or recall can exceed as much as ten years. The longest-lived memories are usually linked to very positive or negative emotional events.*

A cat will respond positively or negatively to a stimulus several years after its occurrence, because cats possess excellent long-term memories. Even though pets learn continuously during their lifetime, they form the most important long-term memories in their early days: 'Puppies and kittens both have periods early in their lives where they learn rapidly about many things in their world. The memories that are formed during this period influence how they behave for the rest of their lives,' says Dr Kersti Seksel, a veterinary specialist of behavioural medicine at Sydney Animal Behaviour Service in Australia. This is why it's so important to expose a kitten to lots of positive experiences and to introduce her to a wide range of people and environments (see page 19), because if she develops an aversion or phobia, it can last a lifetime.

Research over the past few years supports the idea that cats have excellent short- and long-term memories.

Short-term memory: Also known as working memory, its role is to hold information temporarily, in order to allow animals to perform mental calculations using that information. It is vital for reasoning, learning and comprehension. For example, your working memory allows you to phone for pizza and order several pre-arranged items, without having to refer to a shopping list (whilst your long-term memory would allow you to phone the pizza joint without looking up the number, as well as operate the phone and make your order using language). Working memory also enables you to perform mental arithmetic or to plan a journey. You would also expect to forget most of that information within a few seconds or minutes, because you don't need it anymore.

Cats clearly have a good short-term memory, otherwise they would be incapable of any kind of problem-solving and they wouldn't be able to form any long-term memories. As you would expect, a cat's short-term memory excels in tasks that are related to hunting and finding food. In research published recently in the journal *Behavioural Processes*, about 50 cats were tested and were able to remember which containers contained food, or which they had eaten out of, after being taken out of the room for fifteen minutes. Cats were able to retrieve and use the 'what' and 'where' information from a single event.

Long-term memory: This is responsible for the storage of information for an extended period of time, potentially indefinitely. Cats have powerful long-term memories. 'Although a cat might lock only a few people or places into his long-term memory, he can remember them for years. He can remember certain places or people for most of his life,' says cat health expert, Melissa Schindler. There are lots of instances of cats being tearfully reunited with their owners after years of separation, in which it is clear that the cats recognise and remember them.

Age-related memory loss: The good news for cats is that recent studies suggest that they have less of a problem with age-related memory decline than dogs or humans, at least in terms of spatial-learning tasks. In research published in *Applied Animal Behaviour Science*, 36 cats aged 1.0–15.1 years of age were set an identical spatial-learning task (with a control for motor function – i.e. allowing for reduced agility with increased age). No significant age-related decline in cognitive function was found. Bruce Kornreich, the associate director of the Cornell Feline Health Centre, explains: 'Cats don't seem to have the same decline in spatial-learning tasks that humans do'. Although cats can lose some of their cognitive abilities as they age, Kornreich notes, 'in terms of spatial-learning tasks, at least based upon this study, they don't decline in that regard'.

IT'S ALL IN THE
Eyes

Cats have large expressive eyes that not only reveal their emotional state, but the large pupils, and the ratio of photoreceptor cells within the eye, enable them to see in conditions of near darkness. So, although humans have greater visual acuity and can see a wider range of colours, a cat's vision is perfect for all its needs.

A cat's eye has a lens and a retina, just like the human eye, but the major difference is in the ratio of photoreceptors: cones and rods. Cones provide greater colour vision and a sharper image than rods, but they need a lot of light in order to function, whereas rods operate in low light conditions.

A cat's eye has about twenty-five rods to each cone, a higher ratio than a human's one to four, so it only needs about one sixth of the light we need. In daylight, our world is much richer in colour and the landscape is in much sharper focus but this doesn't bother the cat. Its eyesight is perfectly adapted to its feline needs, such as being able to hunt in the dim light of dawn and dusk and detect sudden horizontal movement. David Taylor, in his book *Think Cat*, explains: 'Note how your puss will pounce or strike like lightning at a ball rolling across the floor … [rather than at] objects going up or down … it is instinctively triggered by anything moving over the ground like its natural prey, the scurrying mouse. And mice are rarely to be seen levitating'.

A cat's eye has another feature to help it see in near darkness. It has a special reflective layer behind the retina called the *tapetum lucidum*, which David Taylor engagingly describes as 'a light-intensifying screen composed of up to fifteen layers of cells containing glittering, iridescent crystals'. It reflects light back onto the retina, improving low light vision even further (this is why a cat's eyes glow in the dark).

Cats see best at a distance of two to six metres and their vision is very sensitive to movement. A cat's visual acuity is thought to be about 20/150, which means that if a human with 20/20 vision could see something from 150 feet away, a cat would have to stand 20 feet away to see it as clearly. Cats are longsighted, which means they can't see things very well that are far away, so when you smile

It's All in the Eyes

at your cat from across a large room, she won't be able to see the details of your face but she'll be able to smell and hear you perfectly.

Eye contact is an important part of feline communication and prolonged eye contact is nearly always confrontational. When two cats meet, they will stare each other down to establish which one is dominant. The cat that looks away first loses the showdown. Cats also blink slowly to appease and to tell other cats, 'I am friendly, I mean no harm'. Don't stare at strange cats because they will perceive this as aggression.

> Eye contact is an important part of feline communication

Like puppies, kittens are born with closed eyes and deaf. They usually open their eyes sometime during the second week after birth, so they find their mother's teat by smell alone. All kittens are born blue-eyed and then between the ages of 7 to 12 weeks, melanin determines their permanent eye colour – varied hues of blue and green to rich copper brown.

The shape of the pupils changes with the cat's mood. The vertical slit shape allows them to respond quickly. The pupils turn into narrow slits when a cat is irritated or angry (or if she is exposed to bright sunlight). Wide pupils indicate alertness, such as when you dangle a toy in front of her, or when she is hunting. When she is feeling calm and relaxed, her eyes will be sleepy-looking and half-closed.

Despite the social dominance factor, if your cat is relaxed it's OK to stare lovingly at her, so long as you blink slowly to communicate trust, relaxation and calmness – essentially that you trust her not to attack you while you have your eyes closed. If she slowly blinks back, the feeling is mutual.

TELLTALE *Tails*

A cat's tail is important for jumping and for balance, but when it isn't being used for those things, it is highly expressive in terms of body language, not only to reveal her emotional state but to communicate with humans and other cats.

Telltale Tails

Tails are effective communicators because they can be seen from a long way away, distinct from the rest of the body. This is important when you consider that cats are near-sighted and can't see with great detail things that aren't in their sweet spot of between two to six metres away.

When your cat struts into the room with her tail held vertically, maybe with the tip curled towards her head (the tail tip can move independently), that is an unambiguously friendly greeting, which John Bradshaw describes in *Cat Sense* as 'the key signal'. He confidently states, 'The tail-up sign has almost certainly evolved since domestication, arising from a posture kittens use when greeting their mothers … the posture would have evolved into a signal, one that enabled adult cats to live in close proximity to each other with less risk of quarrelling'.

> The tail-up sign has almost certainly evolved since domestication

If your cat is especially delighted to see you, she might quiver her tail excitedly in a gesture that looks like she is spraying, so it's often called 'mock spraying'. So far so good. As the tail lowers, the further south it goes, the more extreme her emotional state becomes.

If her tail is at 45 degrees, she is feeling ambivalent, and if the tail is horizontal to the body, it could be neutrally friendly, but you would need to look for other visual clues to get the full picture. For example, when her tail flicks back and forth horizontally (or lower) from side to side, it is a sign of focus and/or possible irritation. A cat with a slowly waving tail indicates that she is focused on something, maybe about to pounce on a toy, but, as her anger becomes more intense, the flicking develops into a lashing movement and is a warning that she is about to attack. If you see this body language outside of playtime, beware.

The 'tail down' position must also be interpreted in combination with other factors. Cats lower their tails when stalking prey, but it is also a defensive fear response, which is at its most acute when the tail is down between the hind legs. Tail down and arched is an aggressive stance and you might also observe that the tail is fluffed up, giving the cat the illusion of looking bigger, which is a threatening display designed to scare an antagonist. In this case, aggression supersedes fear as the tail is held closer to horizontal, and fear dominates the closer the tail gets to fully down.

The friendly tail up sign is probably the most important of all the social tail signals because cats use it to communicate their place in the social hierarchy in recognition of the higher social status of the individual to whom is directed, thereby diffusing potentially confrontational situations. This is why kittens display the tail up when greeting their mothers. During a 2009 study of a colony of feral cats in Italy, researchers noted that the tail up sign was most often deployed by non-aggressive cats towards aggressive cats, to communicate their lower status and to signal that they were peaceful.

John Bradshaw describes how one of his former graduate students, Charlotte Cameron-Beaumont, set up an experiment to gain further insight into the meaning and function of 'tail up'. She taped to a skirting board silhouettes cut from black paper of cats with a variety of tail positions, to eliminate other signalling factors such as pheromones or vocalisations. Then she let cats into the room and observed their reactions: 'If the silhouette's tail was up rather than down, the cat was more likely to approach it, and more likely to raise its own tail. Tail-up therefore seems to signal intention, and may even induce an emotional change in the recipient, possibly decreasing any anxiety that the other cat might attack it'.

EXTRAORDINARY
Senses

Recent research has established that the human nose contains about 6 million scent receptors, in roughly 400 types, allowing us to detect at least 1 trillion different odours (we used to think it was only about 10,000). However, the average cat has around 200 million scent receptors, more than 30 times as many as humans, so the richness of a cat's olfactory world is impossible for us to comprehend.

Cats are born blind and deaf, so their sense of smell is vital for their survival in those early days as they use it to locate their mother's teat. Meanwhile, the mother rubs her own scent on her kittens so she can identify them. Exchanging smells is an important part of feline communication. When your cat rubs against your leg, or brushes his face against yours, he is marking you with his scent (see page 72).

Scent is everything to a cat. He uses it to understand which cats have rubbed and scratched or sprayed urine in his territory and how long ago, as well as their gender and place in the social hierarchy. He can tell which ones are liable to be a threat and which are benign. He uses scent to learn precise information about the opposite sex, to help him to locate prey and to test the edibility of food.

> A cat also has a special scent organ located in the roof of his mouth

A cat also has a special scent organ located in the roof of his mouth behind the front teeth called the vomeronasal (or Jacobson's) organ. This allows him to perform the Flehmen Response, by raising his head, opening his mouth and visibly curling back his upper lip to expose his front teeth. He presses his tongue against the roof of his mouth, which sends the smell chemicals into the Jacobson's organ, allowing him to 'taste' the smell to gather information about feline pheromones in the air and to determine the age, sex and reproductive status of the felines in the vicinity.

The word originates from the German 'flehmen', meaning to bare the upper teeth, and also from the Upper Saxon German 'flemmen', meaning to look spiteful. Jacobson's organ is named after a nineteenth-century Danish surgeon who was fascinated by the now redundant human vomeronasal organ.

Tomcats use the Flehmen Reaction more frequently than female cats, but it is common in both sexes and is also performed by wild cats such as lions and tigers. It has been observed in a wide range of species such as horses, zebras, giraffes, goats, elks, snakes, giant pandas and even hedgehogs.

A cat has comparatively few taste receptors on the tongue. Humans have around 10,000 taste buds, dogs have about 1,700, but cats only have around 470. A cat's sense of smell is not only the stimulant for his appetite, it also helps him to detect the safety of his food. Humans and dogs can detect five tastes – sweet, sour, bitter, salty and umami (savoury). The ability to taste bitter and sour allows carnivores to avoid rancid food.

Cats can do this too, but they are thought to be unique among mammals with respect to their inability to taste sweet. Sweetness is attractive to humans because it indicates a source of carbohydrate – for a quick energy boost. Cats don't eat carbs; they exclusively eat meat so they don't need a sweet tooth. They don't eat fruit, so they don't need a sweet receptor to tell them the difference between ripe and unripe fruit. Despite this, some commercial cat foods contain up to 20% carbohydrates such as corn or grains, because it's a cheap ingredient, but it's debatable whether your cat can even digest this and it may be a factor in domestic cats developing diabetes.

Pam Johnson-Bennett points out in her book, *Think Like a Cat*, 'Taste is not the only consideration in your cat's decision to accept or reject food. Smell, texture, size and even the shape of the food are important issues to him'. To avoid creating a finicky eater, she advises, 'feed a variety of flavours from a couple of manufacturers. Feed both dry and canned foods, so your cat is comfortable with different tastes, scents and textures'.

EARS IN ACTION

Kittens are born deaf and hearing is the last of the senses to fully develop. The ear canals begin to open after about two weeks, and it takes about a month before they function properly. But when a cat's hearing is fully developed, she has the widest range of any carnivore and among the best in the animal kingdom.

Ears in Action

A cat's hearing (45Hz to 64,000Hz) spans 10.5 octaves and significantly outperforms dogs (67Hz to 45,000Hz), particularly at the top of the range, while humans hear in the range of (64Hz to 23,000Hz). This means that a cat can detect the squeaking of her mouse prey or some rustling in the grass from several metres away before she even sees it. We wouldn't be able to hear the tiny ultrasonic rodent even if it was screaming in our ear.

In fact, if you were to watch a blind cat playing with a mouse toy, you probably wouldn't be able to tell she was blind, so well could she track its movements through sound and the vibrations detected by her whiskers.

The cat's ear is similar in structure to a human ear and consists of an outer, middle and inner ear. The outer ear includes the cone-shaped pinna (the part you can see, made of cartilage and covered by skin and fur). Cats have 30 muscles to move each ear (humans have six), so not only can a cat rotate its pinnae through 180 degrees, it can move each one independently to precisely control which sound waves are funnelled into the ear canal. When she doesn't respond to your call, rest assured that there is nothing wrong with her hearing!

The middle ear includes the eardrum and a small, air-filled chamber that contains the three tiniest bones in the cat's body: the hammer, anvil and stirrup (malleus, incus and stapes) that vibrate in response to sound waves. The inner ear is a complex structure that includes the spiral-shaped cochlea (for hearing) and the vestibular system (for balance).

> The cat's ear is similar in structure to a human ear

At the outer side of the pinna, where it meets the head, you may have you noticed a little furry pouch. It's called a 'cutaneous marginal pouch' and is commonly known as Henry's pocket, though nobody knows who Henry is. It occurs in a number of species, including weasels, bats and some dogs, but it is most noticeable on a cat. It is thought to help filter lower pitched sounds to allow improved detection of the extremely high-pitched sounds made by a cat's prey.

There are many stories of cats predicting extreme weather and natural disasters after changes in their behaviour were noticed by humans, and a cat's uniquely superior hearing definitely plays a major role in this.

Not only are a cat's ears highly efficient at hearing and for aiding balance, they are very expressive and form part of a cat's intricate body language. In *Total Cat Mojo*, Jackson Galaxy stresses their importance: 'The ears can move subtly, quickly and independently, which is why they are often the most telling aspects of a cat's body language. They can be the first indicator of a cat's emotional state'.

When she is playful, alert and curious, your cat's ears will be pricked and facing forward, and her body will be angled towards the focus of her attention. When she is anxious, she may twitch her ears. If she is irritated or perceives danger, she will move her ears around to listen for threats or flatten her ears against her head. If she gets into a confrontation with another cat, her ears will also rotate backwards to protect them in anticipation of an attack.

However, interpreting the position of your cat's ears isn't always so straightforward. Because they move independently, you may observe each ear doing its own thing. Jackson Galaxy again: 'When each ear is doing something different, the interpretation is more ambiguous … and in that moment, so is your cat's emotional state'.

HOW MANY WHISKERS DOES A *Cat Have?*

Cats have a dozen whiskers on each cheek (mystacial), arranged in four neat rows, about five shorter ones above each eye (superciliary), some more under the chin (mandibular) and on the wrists (carpal) behind the front paws. They provide a cat with lots of sensory information, to navigate his surroundings, hunt effectively and even communicate his emotional state.

The scientific name for whiskers – the stiff tactile hairs that grow out of an animal's face – is 'vibrissae'. Vibrissae are longer and thicker than ordinary hair and the follicles are larger and more deeply embedded in the skin. They contain blood-filled sinus tissues and are surrounded by sensory nerves. The slightest movement at the tip of one of these long whiskers is magnified by leverage and transmitted to the nerves at the other end. Whiskers can even detect changes in airflow, as has been proved by recent studies with rats.

In low light conditions, whiskers complement a cat's sense of sight by providing tactile feedback about the immediate surroundings. They also help your cat measure the size of the space he is in and prevent him from getting stuck in a tight spot – his whiskers tell him whether it's possible for him to squeeze through. An old wives' tale says that if your cat becomes fat, his whiskers will grow longer to accommodate his larger body size. This isn't true.

If you gently touch one of your cat's superciliary vibrissae (where his eyebrows would be, if he had any), you will notice that he closes his eyes. These whiskers provide protection for his eyes, so if his head gets too close to a branch he can quickly change direction or close his eyes before impact, in the same way that humans who are blind or visually impaired might use a cane to detect objects in their path.

'It's all about vibration, airflow and touch,' says Dr Leonie Richards, head of general practice at the University of Melbourne's U-Vet Veterinary Hospital. 'They can detect airflow, which tells them if they're close to a wall or some other object in a dark room. The whiskers on the back of their paws are arranged to make up for short-sightedness – if they've caught prey it gives them an idea of where the prey are in the feet'.

How Many Whiskers Does a Cat Have?

The two upper rows of whiskers on your cat's muzzle move forward and backward, independently of the two lower ones. This makes them very expressive in response to his emotional state:

- *Happy and relaxed:* Whiskers are in a neutral position, drooping down.
- *Attentive:* When something grabs your cat's attention, or when he is hunting, the whiskers sweep forward and fan out and the muzzle may appear slightly plumped up.
- *Fearful, anxious, stressed:* Whiskers move backwards and eventually flatten against the face in extremis.
- *Defensive aggression:* Whiskers pulled back tightly to the face.
- *Offensive aggression:* Whiskers point forward.

Cat whiskers should never be cut, unless it is necessary for a medical procedure. Whiskers are made of keratin, like claws, but they don't contain any nerves outside the skin. While cutting them doesn't cause the cat physical pain, it would cause a lot of emotional distress and disorientation, so it should only be done in an emergency. Don't be tempted even if you think that your cat's whiskers are 'getting too long'. That isn't for you to judge.

> Cat whiskers should never be cut, unless it is necessary for a medical procedure

Whiskers gradually shed and grow back naturally without any help from humans. They also don't contain or retain melanin – the pigment dye that colours skin and hair – so they are generally white. Some black cats are completely black, including their whiskers and paw pads, but many black cats have white whiskers and pink paw pads.

A MEDLEY OF
Meows

Feral cats are less vocal than their domestic counterparts. Adult domesticated cats communicate using a variety of sounds, but they rarely meow at each other. Kittens make a high-pitched mew to call for help or attention from their mothers. But the remainder of the broad bandwidth of meows is reserved for communicating with humans.

In *The Secret Language of Cats*, Swedish associate professor of phonetics Susanne Schotz summarises the rich variety of meows: 'Its sound can be varied and nuanced almost infinitely … My cats have shown me that there are many different meows. The sound exists in countless variations and is used in very different circumstances … A meow can be assertive, coaxing, demanding, inviting, imperious, whining, melancholic, suffering, friendly, brave or undaunted'.

If you are a cat owner, you will know that for all its wonderful nuanced variety, a meow is most often used to gain your attention. What you may not realise is that while some breeds – Siamese, Oriental, Abyssinian – are more vocal than others, the 'mewbosity' of your cat mainly depends on how much you respond to his vocalisations. Although if you own a Siamese cat, you already know that they are probably the most vocal of all the cats, as animal behaviourist Pam Johnson-Bennett celebrates in her book *Think Like a Cat*: 'Siamese cats love to provide running narratives on their daily activities and aren't shy about voicing opinions. Know this and accept it'.

> A meow is most often used to gain your attention

In 1944, New York psychologist Mildred Moelk categorised sixteen sounds used in cat-human and cat-cat communication, which are still relevant today for understanding feline vocalisations. They first appeared in her paper 'Vocalizing in the House Cat: A Phonetic and Functional Study' in the April 1944 *Journal of Comparative Psychology*.

Moelk's work highlighted how cats frequently use repetition to communicate as well as varying the duration, intensity, tone, pitch, roughness, stress and speed of the sound. She organised the vocalisations into three patterns based on how cats formed the sounds:

1. *Murmur Patterns:* consonant made with mouth closed, breath passes through the nose.
2. *Vowel Patterns:* breath passes through the open mouth as it closes.
3. *Strained Intensity Patterns:* voiced breath forced through the mouth, which is held wide open.

An apostrophe (') means an emphasis, most often from inhalation, and a long dash (—) is a sustained sound.

Murmur patterns

Express greeting or satisfaction, e.g. 'hello', 'pay attention to me'

1. Purr ('hrn-rhn-'hrn-rhn)
2. Request or Greeting ('mhrn'hr'hrn)
3. Call ('mhrn)
4. Acknowledgment or Confirmation ('mhng)

Vowel patterns

Requests or complaints, e.g. 'give me', 'please give me'

1. Demand ('mhrn-a'—ou)
2. Begging Demand ('mhrn-a—ou—)
3. Bewilderment ('maou?)
4. Complaint ('mhng-a—ou)

5. Mating Cry – mild form ('mhrn-a—ou)
6. Anger Wail (wa—ou—)

Strained intensity patterns

Arousal or stress, e.g. 'I like' or 'I don't like'

1. Growl (grrrrr)
2. Snarl (aye–a)
3. Mating Cry (ooy-ooy-a)
4. Pain Scream (aye–ee)
5. Refusal Rasp (aye–aye–aye)
6. Spitting (fff-tu)

Cats really do have a medley of meows, something for every occasion, and they learn from their owners that vocalisations get results – meows lead to food, grooming, playtime, or being let in or outside. If you get woken up by loud repeated meows every morning, you taught your cat to do that (or rather he has trained you to get out of bed to the sound of a feline alarm clock). We humans may be linguistically very clever animals, but cats are also smart enough to realise that humans can be taught to respond to a set of meowed instructions.

There's a meow for 'let me out', another for 'let me in', and another for 'feed me' and 'wake up' or 'pleeeease!'. Never forget that meows are reserved for humans; they are rarely used feline to feline but fortunately not every meow is motivated by an urge to control the world. Sometimes a single short meow just means 'Hello. I see that you are there. I am here also'.

BODY
LANGUAGE

When cats communicate with each other they rely on pheromones and body language – facial features, shape of the pupils, position of the ears and whiskers, tail displays and body posture. All these visual cues communicate a cat's mood. You can read much about a cat's intention from its body language, if you know how to interpret it.

Body Language

Before we examine your cat's body language, it's worth reminding ourselves that we humans communicate lots about our emotional state and intentions through our bodies. It's important that you understand the messages that your own body sends, often without your conscious knowledge.

Firstly, there is a huge size difference between you and your cat. When she stands at your feet and looks up at your head, it's tempting to imagine that she might wonder how she came to take up residence with a giant noisy ape or maybe a sentient tree that is also dextrous enough to open tins of cat food. If you want to put her at ease, play or cuddle, then you need to get down to her level or let her climb up so that she can be close to your face.

When your cat has been naughty and you find yourself scolding her – pointless, by the way, as you have probably already learned from past experience that the best way to discourage undesirable behaviour is to ignore it and to reward good behaviour rather than try to dominate physically and verbally – it's frustrating that she always seems to ignore you.

In fact, by withdrawing eye contact and turning her body away, she is not being rude, she is appeasing you, because she doesn't understand why you are shouting and because you are huge! Equally, during a calmer moment, if you want her to come and join you on the sofa, remain relaxed, quiet and still and don't stare at her. Less is more.

Greeting

Friendly cats approach each other with their tails up and then they exchange scents by rubbing their necks, bodies and tails against each other. When you are standing up, your cat can't reach your face, so she will rub against your leg to say hello. It is important that you acknowledge her greeting by stroking her neck or getting down to her level so she can see and scent your face. Every time you greet, you strengthen family bonds.

Relaxed and happy

A relaxed cat is a cat at rest. It seems self-evident, but an anxious cat won't settle down or get comfortable near you, she will tend to prowl around exuding restlessness! A happy cat will lie down, often with her front paws tucked away neatly hidden underneath her body in the 'meatloaf position', with her eyes half closed – the key sign that she is most definitely not on high alert. Her ears are up and facing forwards, whiskers hanging down her face, tail curled up alongside the body. If she feels very secure, she will roll onto her back and expose her belly, which is the ultimate display of trust. Don't assume it's an invitation to start rubbing her belly though. When your cat is finally at rest, let her enjoy a few moments of bliss, rather than always satisfy your urge to cuddle and stroke, no matter how cute and approachable she seems.

The degree to which your cat is curled up is also an indicator of her temperature. Cats only have sweat glands on their tiny feet, so they alter their body shape to regulate their body heat. At temperatures of 70°F or more, there is very little curl, but as the temperature cools, your cat will incline her head and tuck it into her body and draw her feet in, until at 55°F, half her face will be covered by her tail and her feet will be hidden.

Anxiety and stress

When a cat feels anxious, she will crouch down with her head and body low, muscles rigid. Her legs appear ready for action, as she assesses the situation and her body prepares to fight or flee. Both head and tail are tucked into the body, pupils dilate, eyes wide and unblinking and her ears swivel sideways or move around, on high alert for threatening sounds, or they may flatten against the head. Whiskers may be drawn back along the sides of her face.

Whilst she quietly assesses the threat, she will maintain this posture, making herself as small as possible to appear less threatening or less noticeable. She may literally hide her body under or behind an object. As her anxiety increases, she will start to cower and look really miserable. The tail might be rigid against the body or moving slowly side to side at the tip. However, if she is cornered and has no alternative but to fight, her body language will change as her emotions develop from anxiety to extreme fear or anger and she will make herself look bigger (see below).

If you see your cat displaying this body language, offer her verbal and physical reassurance and try to locate the source of her anxiety. There may be a stranger outside (or inside) the house, most likely another cat. What can she see and hear? What in her immediate environment has changed?

If you can't figure out the immediate cause of her anxiety, you may be able to distract her with some hunting play, which will help work off some of her adrenalin. If your household is noisy, ask everyone to quieten down. As her immediate anxiety reduces, her body will soon relax and return to the neutral state, but if the anxiety persists over several hours or days, then you should remain vigilant to activity inside and outside the house and, if necessary, consult your vet to try to figure out what's wrong.

For example, you might discover that several dominant neighbourhood cats have started appearing in your garden, which is your cat's territory. If your cat doesn't want to fight them, just the sight of them through the window could cause her extreme anxiety. You may be able to reduce her anxiety simply by covering up certain sightlines or blocking all or part of a window, so she can't see the intruders. Also, consider that the anxiety may be caused inside the house, especially if you have more than one cat and/or other pets.

Other signs of persistent anxiety include urinating outside the litter tray, diarrhoea, cystitis, constipation or other digestive issues, excessive grooming or scratching, excessive hiding, increased vocalisation, a decrease in appetite and excessive sleeping.

Anger and fear

She will stand tall, back arched, body sideways to the threat, head facing forward (or she might make darting sidelong glances rather than look directly at the aggressor), hair along the tail and back is fluffed up, posture tense, front paw slightly lifted off the ground (ready to attack). All these actions are designed to make her look as big as possible to deter the opponent and prepare for – but also ideally prevent – a physical fight.

The ears are flattened and pointing out to the side or backwards, mouth is open and tense with teeth showing and by now she'll make some vocalisations. By now the tail may be slashing vigorously from side to side.

Focused

When your cat is intently focused on something, she expresses this curiosity with her entire body. Her head, ears and whiskers point forward, her body inclined towards her goal. If she is stalking, her body is low to the ground, with her hind legs retracted underneath and her tail rigid and low, maybe quivering slightly at the tip.

EIGHT THINGS YOU SHOULD KNOW ABOUT YOUR CAT'S

Cats are natural born killers. All domestic cats have the inborn hunting instinct and their bodies are perfectly designed for the job. Here are some interesting facts you may not know about your cat's crepuscular specialty …

Chattering teeth: When your cat stares out of the window at a bird outside he can't get to, his teeth may start to chatter involuntarily. Behaviourists think that this is either a sign of frustration or excitement. Domestic cats and wild cats kill their prey by delivering a 'kill bite' to the back of the neck, puncturing the prey's spinal cord where the skull joins the spine. Cats sometimes use a chattering movement to help them locate this sweet spot, so teeth chattering behind the curtains is thought to be your cat's reflexive attempt to deliver this fatal bite.

Taste buds: Cats have a weak sense of taste and fewer taste buds than humans. Their olfactory system is geared much more towards hunting and detecting prey than savouring the subtle flavours of an opportunistic rodent snack. The smell of the food is more important than the taste, although cats do have a taste receptor which humans lack – for adenosine triphosphate (ATP), the compound that provides energy to drive many processes in living cells and is a signal for meat, which is the only thing that cats need to eat.

Calorie counting: One mouse provides about 30 calories of energy. A domestic cat of average size would need to eat about eight mice every day to survive in the wild. This would mean hunting anywhere up to 30 times a day to obtain his daily meat requirement, although typically this would amount to less than 20% of his waking time.

Extra time: What does your cat do with all the extra time it saves by not having to hunt for its food? He spends the majority of his daytime hours grooming, looking out of the window and dozing. If your cat goes outside, he will do plenty of hunting because that's his instinct, but if he lives exclusively indoors then you should have at least three play hunting sessions each day where you simulate moving prey using a ball, mouse or feather at the end of a string or wand. Each session need only last 10 minutes and should culminate in allowing your cat to catch the prey and have a successful hunt.

Eight Things You Should Know About Your Cat's Hunting

Cute eyes: Cats have the largest eyes relative to their head size of any mammal. Your cat's big round eyes may look cute but that's also because they belong to a highly specialised nocturnal killer, so they need to collect the maximum amount of light. Inside the eye, the retina is six times more sensitive than ours in low light conditions, sacrificing sharpness and colour perception for the ability to see prey in near darkness. Why do cheetahs have smaller eyes relative to their head size? Because they hunt during the day.

Short digestive tract: Cats have a short digestive tract because they don't need the long tract of herbivores and omnivores for digesting plants. A shorter digestive tract is sufficient for digesting meat and it keeps their weight down, so they can run more quickly and jump more easily.

Killer mimic: Cats have been observed making similar noises to their prey just before they pounce. This is thought to either distract the prey or to cover up any rustling sound caused by the cat winding itself up as it prepares to spring.

Hunting is hardwired, eating prey isn't: Ever wondered why your well-fed cat loves hunting and is forever bringing you little rodent and avian gifts, but never bothers to eat what he catches? That's because kittens have inborn hunting and chasing instincts and they hone their hunting skills through play by stalking, ambushing and chasing their littermates. But they will only learn that the caught prey is food if their mother teaches them. If she never brings home rodents to feed to her kittens (which a breeder wouldn't allow anyway pre-vaccination), they don't learn the association between hunting and eating. Once weaned, they are quickly packed off to other homes and spend their lives hunting for sport rather than for food.

GROOMING

Cats are naturally clean and this is why they spend between 30% to 50% of their waking hours grooming. But all cats also need regular grooming by their owners, regardless of the length of their fur.

Self-grooming

This is an integral part of a cat's daily routine and is essential for maintaining good mental and physical health. A cat's tongue is covered with hard, backwards-facing spines called filiform papillae, which act like the bristles of a comb to brush his fur (and also to strip meat from animal bones). He also uses his teeth and comb-like paws during grooming. Brushing his head with his front paws stimulates tiny oil glands that condition the fur and spread the cat's unique scent all over the body.

Self-grooming helps to regulate body temperature (it fluffs the coat up when it's cold and cools the skin through the evaporation of saliva), keeps the coat clean and smooth, stimulates skin circulation and gets rid of parasites, germs and other potentially harmful debris and stimulates new hair growth. Cats also gain a lot of comfort from grooming and will often use it as a displacement activity when they are feeling anxious.

Changes in your cat's self-grooming routine – either compulsive grooming (leading to hair loss and skin lesions) or under-grooming (which could be a sign of arthritis, pain or dental problems) should merit a visit to the vet. Signs of under-grooming include a rough or greasy coat, matting, urine stains or faeces particles, food particles on his chest after meals and bad odour.

Owner grooming

Many cat owners, especially those with short-haired breeds, have no idea that they should be grooming their cats regularly. Not only does your intervention help to keep the coat clean, it helps to strengthen the bond between you because mothers lick their kittens to clean them, provide comfort and help prevent hairballs.

In *The Cat Whisperer*, Claire Bessant says, 'Contorting that extra-supple body, cats can reach almost all parts by twisting and leaning. But by far the best way to get to those inaccessible places ... is to get a friend to help'. This is where you come in. Your grooming is essential to get rid of matted fur and knots that he can't deal with on his own. Not only does it give him a good massage, it releases the areas where the skin was pulled tight by matted hair, which left untreated can become very painful and even cause skin lesions.

Owner grooming also accustoms your cat to being touched all over his body, in a safe and pleasurable context, so when you need to check your cat's health, or visit the vet, he will have a better experience because he is used to being sensitively handled. The other advantage of regularly getting hands-on with your cat is that you learn what his normal body feels like, so that you can spot any anomalies such as injuries or lumps and bumps.

Nail care

Active outdoor cats usually wear down their nails without any help from their owners. Most indoor cats should be able to keep their own claws sharp and trim by using a scratching post, but if they get too long they can curve into the pad of the foot and cause pain and infection. If you decide to trim your cat's claws, it's best to start when he is young. Ask your vet for advice how to do this safely, avoiding the nail pulp in the centre, which contains nerves and blood vessels.

Hold your pet against your body, gently hold the paw between your thumb and index finger, press gently on the top of the toe to reveal the claw and then clip the claw a few millimetres, without going beyond the transparent part.

TEN THINGS YOU SHOULD KNOW ABOUT
Litter Trays

How much do you really need to know about a litter tray, you may well ask? Quite a lot, in fact. It is one of the most important considerations for cat owners. Getting your cat's toileting requirements right isn't rocket science, but there are still lots of ways to go horribly wrong. So here are 10 things you should know:

1. You should have a minimum of one litter tray for each cat in the household plus an extra one. However, feel free to experiment and start off with six litter trays for one cat, in different locations around the house. Your cat can then choose which ones she likes best and you can remove the less popular ones.

2. You may also experiment with lots of different litters, but the first choice should be the one your kitten was using before you brought her home. Also, most cat experts recommend unscented litter because although strong artificial fragrances may make you feel better about having a cat toilet in your bedroom, your cat may find the smell very off-putting.

3. Cats are very clean creatures and they don't want to do their business close to where they eat or sleep, so the litter tray/s should be placed away from these areas, somewhere quiet where she can feel safe. If you have more than one cat, make sure the placement of litter trays does not leave a cat vulnerable to ambush from other cats while using it.

4. In *Total Cat Mojo*, Jackson Galaxy recommends putting litter trays 'in socially significant areas. These are spaces that both the humans and the animals occupy equally' such as the bedroom and the living room. He recognises that this may be a big sacrifice for you, but he argues 'it *will* reduce or help to eliminate peeing that results from territorial insecurity ... Think of it as the lesser of two evils. It's either a litterbox where you don't want it, or pee where you definitely don't want it'.

5. Some owners like to give their cats extra privacy and security by adding a cover, either home made (cardboard box) or shop bought, but see what your cat prefers. Some cats feel anxious using an enclosed litter tray and it can also smell more pungent

Ten Things You Should Know About Litter Trays

inside. Long-haired cats sometimes get a static electric shock when they brush against the cover.

6. The ideal litter tray size is one-and-a-half times the length of your cat, from her nose to the base of her tail. This gives your cat the space to turn around, dig and cover without feeling restricted.

7. Spot clean litter trays daily and completely replace the litter at least once a week. If the tray becomes too dirty, cats may use the floor instead. Don't clean too frequently because your cat doesn't want her toilet to smell of you or disinfectant.

8. If the litter tray itself is well-placed and clean, going to the toilet outside the litter tray is most often a sign of your cat's territorial insecurity, caused by other cats either inside or outside the home. Otherwise, it may be an indicator of illness.

9. It is actually possible to overfill the litter tray. About five centimetres should be sufficient but see what works best for your cat. Your cat's feet may sink into too much litter and long-haired cats don't like to feel it against the hair on their undercarriage.

10. If you want your cat to go to the toilet outside, then once she has had all her vaccinations, you can begin the transition from litter tray to garden by placing an additional litter tray with half soil and half litter near to the door, or else move the existing one closer to the door day by day. The first option is preferable because it gives your cat choice. Finally, you place the litter tray outside and tip the used contents onto soil so that she links going to the toilet with outside. You may decide to keep a litter tray indoors so that she still can go to the toilet during the night, or when the weather is bad.

RUBBING AND
Scenting

Cats have special scent glands under their chins, at the corners of the mouth, on either side of the forehead, at the base of their tail and between the toes. Rubbing and scenting is a very important part of cat behaviour. When two friendly cats meet, they will rub against each other just as your cat will rub against your leg to say hello and mix scent.

Rubbing and Scenting

These scent glands release a highly detailed and unique pheromone that communicates status, marks territory and even advertises sexual availability. Cats will come back to the same favourite spots time and time again to refresh their scent marking, such as entrances to the home or nesting places, areas of high animal traffic as well as territorial boundaries. The latter are especially important because clearly readable signals of status and virility placed on boundaries can often settle border disputes without the need for a potentially life-threatening physical confrontation.

John Bradshaw makes some interesting observations about rubbing in *Cat Sense*: 'The form that the rub takes seems to vary from cat to cat and, despite years of research, I am still uncertain whether there is any significance in which part of the body the cat uses to rub'. He observes that some cats just rub with the side of the head, others use their flank as well as their tail. However, 'many simply walk past without making any contact at all' and a few will put all their effort into scenting an object nearby 'such as a chair leg or the edge of a door' rather than another creature.

If you are a cat owner, you and your home will reek of cat pheromones, so it's a good job humans can't smell them. A cynical explanation of what is happening when your cat rubs against you is that she isn't showing affection but is instead 'claiming you as her property'. This isn't strictly true but it's all rather baffling. While cats like to rub their signature smell on just about everything in the house – furniture, door frames, curtains, humans, discarded clothing and 'even animals that do not understand the significance

> If you are a cat owner, you and your home will reek of cat pheromones

of the ritual and are unlikely to give anything in return', Bradshaw argues that when it comes to scenting other animals rather than objects, 'if the primary motivation for rubbing was to leave scent behind, cats should constantly try to sniff people's legs to discover if any other cat has left its scent there'. He therefore concludes that 'all the evidence points to rubbing, like stroking, as a primarily tactile display'.

There also appears to be a hierarchy of rubbing. When two cats of different sizes meet, the smaller cat usually rubs itself on the bigger cat, which doesn't rub in response. The same thing happens when your cat rubs against your leg, as most of the time you'll be too preoccupied with cooking or finding your car keys to get down on your cat's level and rub your face into the side of her neck, and your cat seems blithely to accept this.

This means that rubbing against our legs must provide its own reward for cats, otherwise they would eventually stop doing it if they expected a predictable response from humans every time. It remains a learned behaviour in so far as a kitten will happily rub itself on older bigger cats, but when it arrives in a new home at the age of about eight weeks, it doesn't immediately get busy with the leg rubbing. Bradshaw observes, 'young cats (especially females) may take several weeks, or even months, to start rubbing on their new owners, as if they need time to work out how best to use this behaviour to cement the relationship'.

So, if a strange cat rubs against you in greeting, it isn't always a sign of affection. She is scent marking and inspecting yours. She's possibly more intent on rubbing and sniffing than inviting you to start energetically stroking her back. If you misjudge her approaches, don't be offended when she sashays away to commune with a door frame instead.

CLUES YOUR CAT
Loves You

Cats are adept at concealing their emotions, and while relationships between cats and humans have not been shaped by 'co-operative evolution' to the same extent as those between dogs and humans, progressive cat care experts such as Jackson Galaxy stress the importance of moving beyond the concept of cat 'ownership' to an 'understanding that you are in a relationship with your cat' and, furthermore, that 'the magic ingredient in all of this is loving – a deep knowledge that your life together is better than your life apart … to love and be loved'.

Many pet owners would readily admit to being deeply uncomfortable with this level of intimacy with their cat or dog and would no doubt label it unhealthy, sentimental, anthropomorphic and unscientific. They might argue that attributing complex drivers such as 'love' to cats is infantilising and irresponsible and that caring for animals demands a certain mature detachment.

> We don't lose our humanity by connecting with animals on a deeper level

The counter-argument is that love is and, always will be, one of the great philosophical mysteries of the human condition. All attempts to define and understand it fail to circumscribe this metaphysical phenomenon. Despite its intangibility, many of humankind's greatest achievements have been motivated by love, so what harm can there be in acknowledging that cats have emotions and are capable of forming strong emotional attachments to other animals, including humans?

We don't lose our humanity by connecting with animals on a deeper level, we enhance it and even develop a respect for the sanctity of all life. But, more importantly, the empathy that this mindset invites you to experience makes you a more responsible carer because you are more motivated to understand your pet's physical and emotional needs. Jackson Galaxy again: 'Releasing ownership and embracing relationship is, to be sure, a scary damn thing. But it is what makes having others in our life the most precious thing'.

We can all agree that cats have a reputation for being undemonstrative, but they show their love for humans in lots of ways:

__Brings you gifts:__ Whether it's dead animals or toys, it's a sign that she loves and trusts you.

Clues Your Cat Loves You

Grooms you: Familiar cats groom each other as a bonding and social behaviour, to reinforce status and relieve stress. If your cat enjoys grooming you, usually licking your face and hair, or just nibbling you, it's a big sign of trust and affection. A cat will only do this if she feels very safe and comfortable with you and has a strong bond.

Head bunting: Your cat nudges her face against yours, or another part of your body, using scent glands on her forehead and face to deposit scent on you. As Pam Johnson-Bennett explains in *Think Like a Cat*, 'This is typically an affectionate behaviour and probably has more to do with bonding than marking'.

Purring: In most circumstances, purring is a good indication that your cat loves hanging out with you. They purr to calm themselves when they are in pain, but they reserve their purrs exclusively for humans they love and they don't purr for other cats, except their own kittens.

Says hello: Simply trotting into the room with her tail held high, maybe with a little curl at the tip, then rubbing herself against your leg is a big hello to one of her favourite people. Don't ignore this flattering sign of how she feels about you. Bend down and let her scent your hand or get down to her level and let her scent your face.

Shows you her belly: Cats only show their vulnerable bellies voluntarily to those they trust and feel affection for, although it's usually not an invitation to rub her there.

Slow blink: Cats usually view eye contact as confrontational, but if your cat is relaxed and contented, she may gaze at you and then slowly blink. This signals that she loves and trusts you not to attack her while her eyes are closed. You can send her back a slow blink eye kiss to tell her the feeling is mutual.

PROBLEM
Behaviour

It is important to allow your cat to engage in normal feline behaviours, otherwise he will start to display dysfunctional behaviour that indicates that his daily needs are not being met. Normal behaviours include hunting, eating, drinking, elimination, play, exploration, climbing, perching, scratching, grooming, sleeping and feeling safe.

Problem Behaviour

As we have already seen in earlier chapters, 'The most common feline behaviour problems are associated with elimination', says Gary M Landsberg of the North Toronto Veterinary Behaviour Specialty Clinic. 'Some of these are related to the litter box, while others reflect social conflicts and involve anxiety or aggression. Much feline aggression is subtle and passive, so its real frequency may be greatly underestimated'.

It may seem obvious, but it's worth bearing in mind that whatever your cat is doing that has come to your attention, it is a sign that he has a problem that can only be fixed with your help, otherwise he would already have resolved it on his own. It requires your active intervention and a proactive approach in order to do the best for your cat. You can't just cross your fingers and hope that time will sort things out. This lazy attitude is especially common when two cats in a household don't get along and the owner does nothing in the mistaken belief that the cats will eventually work it out amongst themselves (usually to the detriment of one of the cats).

> You can't just cross your fingers and hope that time will sort things out

Here are five common behavioural problems and a brief overview of what might cause them:

Elimination in the wrong place: Once the litter tray itself has been ruled out as a cause (e.g. too dirty, too clean, in the wrong place), most litter tray issues are territorial – a threat or perceived threat from another cat or cats, either inside or outside the house.

Scratching in the wrong place: First, make the place where he is scratching unappealing. For example, if he has been scratching the arm of the sofa, temporarily cover it with tin foil, double-sided sticky tape or a polycarbonate chair mat. Second, consider the appeal of the scratching post. Is your cat seeking something by scratching the sofa that he can't get from the post (e.g. the post might be too short or wobbly). Fix those problems. Then move the scratching post so that it is next to the scene of the crime – in this case the sofa – then take off your shirt and rub it against the post, to transfer your scent. Praise him and give him treats whenever he uses the post.

Spraying: This is usually caused by anxiety and environmental stress, such as moving into a new home, a change in routine, absences from home or inappropriate punishment. It is common in multiple cat households. Spraying marks territory, so anything that stresses your cat out can be the cause. Figure out what changes in the household occurred immediately prior to the start of the spraying behaviour and at the time of each subsequent occurrence.

Biting or scratching humans: After you have ruled out a medical cause, the simple act of keeping a detailed diary of every incident will help you to establish patterns and begin to figure out why it is happening. In the meantime, make sure you are having plenty of healthy positive interaction with your cat, especially using structured play, rather than punishing her by avoidance.

Cats don't get along: The main source of tension in a multiple cat household is competition for resources. In *Think Like a Cat*, Pam Johnson-Bennett advises: 'The first rule is to make sure there's enough of everything for everybody. No one should have to share a litter box, food bowl, scratching post, bed or toy if they don't want to'. To break up a fight, bash a saucepan to make some startling noise. At other times, when you can feel tensions rising, use interactive toys to distract and redirect your cats' aggression before they take it out on each other.

STRESS, ANXIETY AND
Depression

Until fairly recently, many scientists have been reluctant to accept the idea that cats might have an emotional life similar to humans, or even to acknowledge their ability to feel pain in any meaningful way. Fortunately, there is now a wide consensus that cats experience anxiety and stress and that they can and do suffer from depression.

In *Cat Sense*, John Bradshaw states: 'the most common cause of anxiety in cats is probably the worry that their territory is likely to be invaded by other cats in the neighbourhood, or even by another cat in the same household'. He surveyed 90 cat owners in suburban Hampshire and rural Devon and 'they reported that almost half of their cats regularly fought with other cats, and two out of five were fearful of cats in general'. His colleague, veterinary surgeon Rachel Casey, who specialises in cat behavioural disorders, 'regularly diagnoses anxiety and fear as the main factors driving cats to urinate and defecate indoors, outside the litter tray', as well as spraying on the walls or furniture to deter other cats. Anxiety also presents in many other ways including hiding, incessant meowing, aggression, excessive grooming, hair loss and shaking.

> Almost half of their cats regularly fought with other cats

Bradshaw goes on to highlight the clear link between stress and anxiety and urinary tract infections such as cystitis and he says that as many as two thirds of cats taken to vets for a range of urination problems 'have no obvious medical problems' and that the triggers are psychological.

This prevalence of urinary problems in the domestic cat population with no apparent medical cause has baffled the veterinarian community for years, but the work of Dr Tony Buffington, Emeritus Professor of Veterinary Clinical Sciences at Ohio State University, indicates that Bradshaw's analysis is correct.

Buffington has treated hundreds of animals that have developed chronic illnesses that he attributes to anxiety and stress. He has even suggested a name for this phenomenon, which he calls 'Pandora

Syndrome'. He led research involving 32 cats over a period of three years and studied other clinical research from the past two decades and concluded that urinary problems in cats occur due to 'complex interactions between the bladder, nervous system, adrenal glands, husbandry practices, and the environment in which the cat lives'. He has also discovered that these animals can be restored to health, not with antibiotics, but by reducing the stressors within their home environment.

Buffington is particularly passionate about the need for indoor cats to have enriched environments to compensate for their inability to hunt and patrol territory outdoors. One ingenious solution is offered by Jackson Galaxy in *Total Cat Mojo*. Galaxy believes that cats should be kept indoors (so long as we 'replace the perceived loss of quality by involving ourselves in our cat's lives more'). He suggests creating a 'Catio' which he describes as 'basically a space that you can make for cats (which of course you can share with them) by enclosing your existing patio or creating an enclosure. There you can offer great vertical spaces, wooden objects that they can scratch on, different grasses, including catnip [nepeta] ... even hunting that can happen when critters make their way inside'.

Chronic anxiety and depression in cats are linked to the same chemical deficiencies in the brain as in humans, including a lack of the neurotransmitter serotonin and an excess of the stress hormone cortisol. But external stressors such as bereavement, separation, moving house, a new baby or pet, illness, injury or abuse, can all cause depression in cats, which often presents as physical illness. Behavioural symptoms of depression in cats are very similar to those in people. A depressed cat will become withdrawn and lose interest in all the things he once enjoyed, and his eating and sleeping habits often change.

SIGNS YOUR CAT IS *Unwell*

Cats can't use words to tell us that they are sick, so they can only let us know through physical symptoms and changes in behaviour. You know your cat better than anyone else, so if you have any suspicions about their health, however seemingly trivial, trust your instincts and speak to your vet.

Signs Your Cat is Unwell

First, it's worth noting that your cat may be living with pain without your knowledge. 'If an animal is in pain or unwell, it attempts to hide all outward signs of discomfort for fear that this weakness will encourage a rival to drive it away,' says John Bradshaw in *Cat Sense*. 'In solitary animals such as cats, exaggerated displays of emotion are therefore unlikely because evolution would have selected out these behaviours'.

Veterinary technician and hospital manager Jenna Stregowski gives another reason why cats and many other animals do not show their pain: 'they simply do not have an emotional relationship with their discomfort. Animals tend to accept the pain or illness as the new normal and move on. It may not be until they are extremely ill that their sickness becomes obvious to humans'.

> Animals tend to accept the pain or illness as the new normal and move on

The best way to tell if your cat is ill is to be alert to a variety of subtle changes in behaviour, however small. *Feline Behaviour Guidelines*, issued by The American Association of Feline Practitioners, advises: 'In cats, physical illness and pain are most often recognized on the basis of a *non-specific change in behaviour*'.

Your cat may be more subdued than normal, sit in a hunched position, might not lift his head properly, carry his tail in a different way, hide away and have stiff body movements, be unwilling to move or display uncharacteristic aggression.

The top 16 signs that your cat may be ill

1. Behavioural changes, especially hiding away.
2. Appetite change (has not eaten properly for 24 hours), unexplained weight loss or gain.

3. Litter tray issues.
4. General lethargy, reduction in energy/activity level, lack of interest.
5. Frequent vomiting or change in bowel movements.
6. Blood in urine, stool or vomit.
7. Diarrhoea or constipation.
8. Excessive drinking or urination.
9. Lameness or stiffness.
10. Bad breath, drooling, panting.
11. Skin complaints, hair loss, sores, lumps.
12. Coughing, sneezing, laboured breathing.
13. Dry, red or cloudy eyes.
14. Discharge from eyes or nose.
15. Change in gum colour from usual healthy deep pink.
16. Dehydration: gently grip his skin near his shoulder blades, pull it up and away from him, then let go. If he is well hydrated, the skin should snap back into place immediately.

The symptoms of poisoning aren't always obvious

Signs Your Cat is Unwell

The above symptoms are all signs of underlying illness, but you should also be alert to injuries that require emergency treatment, such as snake bites, poisoning, etc. The symptoms of poisoning aren't always obvious, but they commonly include confusion, drooling, vomiting, fitting/seizures and difficulty breathing.

Snake bite: The first signs of a snake bite usually include restlessness and excessive panting and drooling, although you might be able to locate the bite through redness, bleeding or swelling. Get your cat to the emergency vet immediately. If the snake is poisonous, your cat may experience vomiting, diarrhoea, shock, collapse, seizures and sometimes paralysis while you are rushing him for treatment.

Poisoning: Dozens of house and garden plants are poisonous to cats, as well as other common hazards around the home such as milk (most cats are lactose intolerant and milk will upset their stomach), chocolate, grapes, raisins, onions, garlic, chives, leeks, avocado, alcohol, coffee beans, raw dough, dog food, blue cheese, macadamia nuts, xylitol (artificial sweetener found in sugar-free gum, bread and other baked goods), raw meat, almonds, walnuts, pistachios, pecans, Niger bird seeds, slug pellets, human drugs (and anything mouldy so keep your cat away from your food waste bin). Some of those ingredients may surprise you but this list is by no means exhaustive, so spend half an hour now on the internet to brush up your knowledge. It could save your cat's life.

> Dozens of house and garden plants are poisonous to cats

ELDERLY CATS

In her book Modern Cat Health, *Dr Sarah Brown mentions some of the many changes that old age can bring a cat, both physical and behavioural: 'Physically they may begin to suffer from dental decay, failing eyesight and hearing, stiffness in the joints and other classic "old age" problems … Behaviourally, elderly cats may become more affectionate toward their owners or quite the opposite'.*

Scientists now use epigenetics – the study of changes in organisms caused by modification of gene expression – to gain a more accurate picture of how animals age in comparison to humans. It appears that cats and dogs age very rapidly in the first two years and slow down as they get older.

The formula for calculating the equivalent age is fairly simple: the first two years of a cat's life equate to 24 human years and every year thereafter is equivalent to 4 human years. For example, a 14-year-old cat would be equivalent to a 72-year-old human.

Cats are considered to be senior once they reach 11 years and their needs usually change from this age. Cats over the age of 15 are classed as super-senior. Some cats can reach this age without showing any signs of being so old, but here are some important tips to keep your 11+ year old cat happy and healthy:

Dental health: Look after their teeth and gums. Tartar build-up in cats can have a lot of negative results.

Diet: Good nutrition from birth is important for a long and healthy life, but it becomes especially important in the later years. Typically, senior cat food will still provide high quality protein, but contain fewer calories to help your cat to maintain her optimum weight despite a decrease in activity levels. Many senior cat foods have some added ingredients to boost the immune system and help the joints, such as vitamin E. Consult your vet about your own cat's specific requirements and whether you should switch to a senior food.

Exercise: Just because your cat is old, it doesn't mean she shouldn't have regular exercise, so long as she is in good health. She may not be as agile as she used to be, but regular exercise helps to maintain muscle mass and reduces the likelihood of obesity.

Feline Cognitive Dysfunction: It's estimated that cognitive decline – feline cognitive dysfunction, or FCD – affects more than 55% of cats aged 11 to 15 years and more than 80% of cats aged 16 to 20 years. This negatively impacts memory, learning ability and sight and hearing perception. This will present itself in many different ways as it can affect a wide range of abilities. If you notice some of these symptoms, speak to your vet about a possible diagnosis of FCD: eliminating outside the litter tray, near eating or sleeping areas; sometimes unable to recognise familiar people and pets; stares fixedly; wanders aimlessly; can't navigate around or over obstacles (with no apparent physical cause); reduction in appetite; reduced personal care; reduced activity and motivation; increased anxiety and irritability; increased vocalisation; disrupted sleep – sleeps more during the day, more restless and vocal at night.

Obesity: Aging is typically associated with lower energy expenditure and the tendency to gain fat and lose muscle, but it is important to maintain your cat at a healthy weight. Obesity puts more stress on the joints and it's associated with a range of health problems, just as with humans.

Temperature control: Older cats are typically more sensitive to extreme temperature changes because of changes in their metabolism. They are less able to thermoregulate, just like older humans, especially if reduced mobility makes it harder for them to groom themselves.

For more information about caring for a senior cat, see *Complete Care for Your Aging Cat* by renowned animal behaviour consultant, Amy Shojai, which is 'filled with heart-warming stories of successful senior citizen cats' as well as 'comprehensive cat reference material from interviews with over 100 veterinary experts'.

TWENTY THINGS YOU SHOULD KNOW
About Cats

How much do you really know about the wily felid on your sofa? Here are 20 fun facts to keep you on your toes, rather like your cat, who is a digitigrade, which means he stands or walks on his toes and the bones of his feet make up the lower part of the visible leg.

Catology

1. Cat claws curve downward, which is why cats can only climb down trees by walking backwards.
2. Response to catnip (nepeta) is hereditary. About 70% to 80% of cats go crazy for catnip and it also affects lions, tigers and leopards.
3. Neutered males live an average of 60% longer than unneutered cats and spayed females live an average of 40% longer than unspayed cats.
4. Indoor cats live on average for about 17 years, while outdoor cats live an average of between 2 to 5 years.
5. When your cat sticks his backside in your face, it is a gesture of friendship.
6. On average, puberty, or sexual maturity, occurs in cats at about five or six months of age, but cats can get pregnant at the age of 4 months.
7. Cats purr at a frequency of between 25 and 150 Hz. Sound frequencies in this range have been shown to promote healing and improve bone density.
8. Some cats love the taste of tuna so much that they refuse to eat anything else. Tuna cannot provide all of a cat's dietary requirements, so a tuna-addicted cat will end up suffering from malnutrition.
9. A cat can jump six times its length in a single bound.
10. The chemical in catnip that makes most cats go crazy for it is called nepetalactone. Cats only respond to catnip after they have reached sexual maturity.

Twenty Things You Should Know About Cats

11. A study published in *Animal Behaviour* tested 42 cats – 21 male and 21 female – for paw dominance and determined that it is correlated with gender: female cats tend to be right-pawed, male cats left-pawed.

12. You should always cook fish before serving it to your cat. Uncooked fish can contain bacteria that causes food poisoning and an enzyme that destroys thiamine, an essential B vitamin, leading to neurological problems.

13. For 20 years, an orange tabby cat called Stubbs was the mayor of Talkeetna, a small town in Alaska.

14. Cats walk using a 'pacing gait', like camels, brown bears and giraffes, by moving both of their right feet first, then both of their left feet.

15. A cat's walk is much less energy-efficient than a dog's, which means dogs are much better at walking long distances.

16. Cats can drink sea water to survive.

17. Each cat's nose print is unique, like a human fingerprint.

18. Cats' sweat glands are only found on their paws. During hot weather, if your cat's paws feel damp, that's sweat.

19. Isaac Newton did not invent the cat flap in the door of his study at Trinity College, Cambridge. The earliest known version of this urban myth appears in an essay in 1802, in which Newton was a wise fool for cutting two holes – one for the mother cat and a smaller, unnecessary hole for her kittens.

20. Kittens in the same litter can have more than one father, because a female cat releases several eggs over the few days that she is in heat.

WHAT CAN WE LEARN FROM CATS?

Over millennia, cats have been worshipped and persecuted in equal measure. They have had temples built in their honour and they have been tortured and killed. They have a reputation for resilience that is literally mythical – they don't have nine lives and they don't always land on their feet. But our cats can certainly teach us daily lessons about how to live our lives.

What Can We Learn From Cats?

Have a curious spirit: Although a cat's curiosity can sometimes lead her into harm's way, when she is outside, she doesn't shy away from existing on the boundary of her comfort zone. 'Curiosity killed the cat' warns of the dangers of unnecessary inquisitiveness, but the origin of that proverb was 'care'll kill a Cat' (first recorded in Ben Jonson's play *Every Man in His Humour*, 1598).

Make sleep a top priority: Your cat knows better than anyone that she just can't function properly unless she is well rested. She literally invented the cat nap and, despite snoozing for between 12 and 16 hours a day, she still manages to lead a busy active life, full of adventure.

Always look your best: Your cat can spend as much as half her waking time grooming herself or others, but not because she is vain. It stimulates circulation, reduces stress, regulates body temperature and keeps her coat clean and knot-free by distributing natural skin oils. In other words, she looks good *because* she prioritises her health.

Be present: Aside from the fact that a cat can sleep up to 16 hours a day, when she is awake she lives in the moment and is fully present to her surroundings. She doesn't worry about the past or the future and so, unlike many humans, she is unburdened by imaginary fears.

Be an explorer: Even though she is a cautious animal, as a born hunter and explorer, she recognises that sometimes you have to take a few calculated risks to reach the heights and see the sights others only dream about.

Play: All cats love to play and they throw themselves into it with absolute focus. We know how important it is for our pet cats to play every day, while we humans often tend to neglect our own play and prioritise everything else. Cats know that regular play keeps mind and body limber and helps you to feel young.

Eat more fish: Fish is one of the healthiest foods on the planet. A healthy, balanced human diet should include at least 2 portions of fish a week, including one of oily fish. That's because fish and shellfish are good sources of many vitamins and minerals. Oily fish are a rich source of long-chain omega-3 fatty acids, which are good for your heart.

Stretch regularly: It is no coincidence that one of the core yoga stretches is *Marjariasana* – the cat posture – a gentle back bend that brings flexibility to the spine, strengthens wrists and shoulders, massages the digestive organs, tones the abdomen, improves blood circulation and relaxes the mind.

Teach people how to treat you: Cats gain our respect because they don't let anyone push them around and they won't settle for second best. If something in their world is out of kilter – water bowl in the wrong place, litter tray needs cleaning – they let us know about it and they don't let up until we take responsibility to fix the problem.

Be independent: While they share our home, they are happy enough to eat the delicious fare that comes out of those little tins, but, if all this ended tomorrow, cats can always fend for themselves. However, they are smart enough to know when they are onto a good thing, so while the going is good, they aren't afraid to just go with the flow.

Single-mindedly pursue your goals: Cats know what they want and need, and they will stubbornly persist until they get it (as anyone who has been woken up by their cat at 6:00am demanding breakfast knows all too well). When they are hunting, they give complete focus to the task and, if at first they don't succeed, they never give up.